BORN
FOR
THIS
PURPOSE

JOAN HOLMES-RADFORD

BORN FOR THIS PURPOSE

*A mother's journey through the
grief process and how God
prepared her son for this day
and how faith and the lessons
God taught her has brought
comfort and peace*

PHILIPPIANS 4:7 (NKJV)

Xulon Press
2301 Lucien Way #415
Maitland, FL 32751
407.339.4217
www.xulonpress.com

Printed in the United States of America.

ISBN-13: 978-1-66280-052-8

TABLE OF CONTENTS

Preface

Isaiah 55: 8-9 NKJV

8: For my thoughts are not your thoughts, neither are your ways my ways, declares the Lord.

9: For as the heavens are higher than the earth, so are my ways higher than your ways and my thoughts than your thoughts.

Philippians 4: 7 NKJV

7: And the peace of God, which passeth all understanding, shall keep your hearts and minds through Christ Jesus.

As a grieving mother, one thing I have learned and held in my heart is:

God's decisions are perfect, even though we don't understand them. He knows the future…we don't. He has a higher purpose than we can understand.

A SPECIAL THING I HAVE COME TO KNOW THROUGH THE STILL SMALL VOICE OF THE HOLY SPIRIT…MY SON WAS BORN FOR THIS PURPOSE.

As you read the pages of this book, you will understand why I say this.

This book will detail the evening my family learned of my son's death. It will tell of our family's reactions. As the story progresses, it tells of our trip to his home and all the questions and conversations during the time from Barry's death to the day of his funeral.

The next section of the book discusses his upbringing, high school, and college days. The book continues, telling of his marriage and life with his wife and children. Finally, my journey through grief is discussed through the mental evaluation of all the things that transpired throughout his life and how so many events in his life brought him to the person he became and how God prepared him and his family for his last day on earth. It will tell of the many thoughts God gave me that helped me to understand His sovereignty and to begin to have a degree of peace.

PRELUDE:

I DO NOT WISH TO EXCLUDE ANYONE SUF-fering from the death of a dear one, but this is my story. It is the story of my long journey down the long trail of grief. I am a Christian and this is being told from that vantage point. It is my hope that readers will be able to gain understanding of their feelings, and somewhat relate to the many stages I have been through and am still going through. A non-believer would not be able to get comfort from much of what I have to say. Still, you are invited to read on. My son, Robert Barry Roberson, almost 3 years ago (as of this writing), suddenly dropped dead of either a heart attack, or an embolism (as paramedics thought). Hopefully, as I get to the story of my son's adult life, any grieving reader will find comfort and peace through his life's experiences. His story will follow my journey of grief.

This story includes passages showing God's intervention in events and decisions. It tells of miracles in Barry's life. Further, this book includes the journey, step by step whereby our Lord brought him to the exact place He wanted Barry to be, right up until He took my son, Barry Roberson, or allowed him to be taken.

CHAPTER

1

WHAT IS GRIEF?

THROUGH THE EXPERIENCE OF LOSING A child, this is what I perceive grief to be:

Grief, that terrible emotion that steals from its victim and strips the victim of happiness and joy, even energy…at least for a season. Grief cripples one's ambition, drive, hope for a future in the early stages, and often robs one, for months and sometimes years to come, of the desire to go on. Thankfully, most of the toll grief takes on its victims is not everlasting, though there are aspects one feels will never end.

Grief…such a tiny word to convey so much diversity of emotion. The denotation of the word is pretty simple, yet the connotation can take on so many forms. The following is what I have found, from experience, grief to be. Every experience with grief is different. When we tell someone we feel their grief, we usually mean that we feel a heaviness of heart for them. Do we feel the same heaviness they do? NO. We might feel a weighty feeling and a short-lived emotion, while that person feels as though an anvil has been looped around the very heart and is pulling down, breaking their heart into pieces.

There are so many types of grief. There is the loss of a parent, the loss of a sister or brother, the loss of a child, or the loss of a dear friend. Each brings with it a different degree of suffering. Each person who suffers any one of those losses, suffers that loss differently. Each relationship is different. For example, if a Christian lady loses a husband who is a professed non-believer, she would live with the agony of knowing she will never see him again and possibly be tormented by thoughts of him in a burning hell. I am just being frank in considering what might go through a person's mind. Of course the degrees of agony would depend on what a person believes or perceives life to be about. One parent who loses a child to death might be extremely close to that child and might feel a deeper loss than a parent who has had little contact with a child over the years and perhaps had not as great a capacity for love and consequently, had a failed relationship. A Christian parent who knows their child has made provisions for eternity by accepting Christ can experience deep grief in knowing they can't see that child again until they also go to be with Christ, or Christ returns, but they have the joy in knowing they will see that son or daughter again one day. Yes, that parent has a mixed concoction of emotions. They experience both sorrow and joy. You can see where I am going with this. It has been my experience advancing through my journey with grief that no one is able to completely identify with your grief if you are the grieving party.

One of the hardest things to hear when you lose a dear one to death is, "I know how you feel." Your heart is telling you, "No you don't! No one knows how I feel." Actually, they don't unless they have had an identical relationship with the person they lost and the one they lost was the same relative (husband, son, daughter, mother, father, etc.}. That is not likely. Your friends and acquaintances mean well, but it is upsetting to hear. Of course, there are certain emotions all grieving individuals have in common. Still, I have heard several grieving people express that they feel "turned off" by the particular comment discussed above. It is important to graciously say to well-wishers, "Thank you" and move on. You must understand, that if the well-wisher has never had this kind of experience, they just can't understand and they feel they are being sympathetic. I know. I was once only a well-wisher to the grieving.

Among the innocent remarks people make when a child is taken is this one, "I know it is not supposed to be this way...your child is not supposed to "go" before you do." Again, a well-meaning remark and in the past, I might have offered that as condolence. Although, after having lost my son, though I loved friends for trying to be comforting, sometimes it is hard not to think...but NEVER say, "Of course, we would not expect them to go first. Maybe that's not the way it is *supposed* to be, but that's the way it IS." While in a state of grief, some statements just don't "set" right. However, it is important to remember, they are just trying to help.

One of the most comforting statements I can recall, was a very honest remark that a friend made, realizing and verbalizing to me that she knew there were no words to remove the pain, that she was just so sorry. Then she shared a few wonderful remarks about her memories of my son. I don't think there is anything that blesses the heart more than shared memories of one's loved one, God has taken.

Then, lastly, you might find that people you know will tend to avoid you in stores, or in restaurants, or even in the workplace upon your return. Often, they fail to make eye contact. It is my assumption that they don't know what to say. I can't say that I don't understand. I have been guilty of the same behavior in days past. Acquaintances, especially if only that (and were never close friends), just don't know if expressing sympathy will only make you feel worse, or cause you to break down and cry, or if it could bring consolation. So...more often than not, they just avoid you. Try not to take offense. Just give them time and realize they are not trying to be unkind.

I'll never forget a remark made by a growing up friend about 4 months after my son died and I had just found out my daughter had cancer. I had tried to get back into choir and the Christmas Cantata was coming up. The Sunday we were to present the Cantata, the lady (having no idea how it would affect me, intending no harm) said to me, just as we were walking out, "I know this is your first Christmas without Barry." The tears I was already fighting broke loose. I had to walk down out of the choir and to a seat in the congregation. Those tears became a flood of tears and, finally, I had to excuse myself and go home. I totally lost control. She was trying to be sympathetic and I do not resent her for the remark, I know she had no desire to upset me, but it was more than I could deal with. I was already worried about whether or not I could contain myself in lyrics in some of the songs where it expressed that God gave his only son. Barry was my "only" son. Hopefully, none of my readers would make that kind of mistake.

A similar situation arises when a spouse passes away. Suddenly, friends tend to avoid inviting you to affairs which involve couples. After a while, you might not be invited over to play bridge, or you might not be invited to a dinner party. There will be adjustments. Some of those adjustments hurt. Your old friends do not intend to cause you pain. Often, the fact is, they don't know how to accommodate the altered situation. Also, as hard as it may sound, sometimes wives do not wish to have available women around their husbands. I realize you don't feel like an "available" woman, but, in reality, that is what you have become in the eyes of some people. The reverse might be true of a grieving man over his deceased wife. People have different ways of adapting. I remember how my mother used to tell me I had to use "mind over matter." Some may resort to that in trying to face reality. Just be careful to rely on the "…mind which is Christ Jesus!"

Some churches have grief classes which are designed to help grieving parties to understand changes and adapt themselves to these changes. I attended one such class, and found that it helps, more than you would think, to be able to talk about your loved one whom the Lord has taken, and to discuss similarities in your thinking. One thing I recall is thinking about the first time I laughed out loud after I lost my son. A month or so had passed. The old," I Love Lucy" show came on the channel I had on, but was not really watching, as my thoughts were all about my son. Lucy's antics caught my attention. She did something exceedingly funny, whereupon I burst out laughing. I caught myself immediately and felt guilty and ashamed. How could I laugh when my son was gone. To my surprise, when I got up the nerve to share that experience with the group, I found that a couple of other people had had the same experience. All this time I thought something must be seriously wrong with me and my responses to a life changing experience. These classes really do help.

CHAPTER

2

PRAYERS AND EARLY INTERVENTIONS

FROM THE DAY EACH OF MY FOUR CHIL-
dren was born, I experienced a certain degree of
worry. I prayed for each and depended on my Lord
to protect them. As they grew into the teenage years,
concerns became greater. Sometimes I would enter-
tain thoughts of the horror of a knock on the door,
or a phone call that would change life for the family
forever. Immediately, I would call on God to put His
protective hedge around them, then I would shake
the thoughts and leave it in His hands. Different
ones of my children were involved in car accidents
which could have been fatal, *several* times…each

time… the Lord intervened. There were other incidents involving danger that God took control over and kept them from harm. Once they had survived the teenage years and had grown into young adulthood, I relaxed somewhat, but still prayed daily for their safety. Barry, in particular, totaled at least two vehicles (one crushed so that even the law officials were surprised he survived with only a cut on his head which required stitches). In another situation, the car left a curve on a foggy night when the curve was not visible, flipped (tearing down a fence) and landed right up against a tree, upside down. He barely had a scratch! Another couple of inches over and the driver's side would have hit the tree square on. I know the angels were guiding the car.

Perhaps one of Barry's experiences that haunted me for years was one involving a shooting. Barry and one of his friends were riding around one night with a couple of other friends. The driver had a gun, but was taking gun safety classes and was very careful to empty and clean his gun after each practice. The story told to me by another parent is that the driver clicked the gun at Barry and the guy beside him in the back seat just "playing around." They had stopped to get gas when another classmate…and friend… saw them and was walking over to talk when he saw the driver get out and noticed he had the gun in his hand. Playfully, the approaching teen threw up his hands and said, "Shoot me, man, shoot me!" The young man knew in his mind the gun was empty. The driver, also feeling complete assurance that the gun was empty, pulled the trigger. The gun went off, shooting the boy in the heart. He died. This was a traumatic experience for all involved, needless to say. Actually, it was comparable to Russian Roulette. It could have been any of the three. There was no excuse for playing with a gun. It was a senseless killing. I am sure that the driver was very sure, in his mind, that the gun was empty. I have always wondered if the younger brother might have gotten into his older brother's car and put a bullet into one chamber. Barry said there were bullets spilled all in the back seat. We will never know why this happened, but I do know that God was sparing both the other boys for a greater purpose. The "backseat friend" is active in his church also and works with youth.

In years to come, some of my grandchildren were in wrecks which totaled vehicles, but they came out with only minor injuries. I suppose, over the years, I had begun to feel that, for some reason I could not understand and knew I did not deserve, that God's favor was on my family and nothing bad could happen. I almost became a little arrogant in thinking God would NEVER let anything happen to my children or me. Still, I prayed daily for their safety. As they became middle-aged, I learned some of them had very high cholesterol and some high blood pressure, I began to be concerned. Yet, again, I prayed, shared bits and pieces of health information (which they largely ignored) and left it in God's hands.

CHAPTER

3

DECISION DIRECTED BY GOD

FAST FORWARD TO JULY 31, 2017. MY daughter, Mary Elizabeth had come to visit a couple of days before the events that would ensue, from Colorado. She sometimes would fly into Atlanta and rent a car. She said even with the rental it was significantly less expensive. From Atlanta, she would drive to Live Oak. When she came, her favorite place to vacation was St. Augustine. On this occasion, she and I and her two daughters had traveled to Siesta Keys for a beach volleyball tournament in which one of her daughters would be playing. She only had little over one day left upon returning to Live Oak, before her return flight to Colorado. My granddaughter, Dara was married and lived in Ft. Walton Beach. Mary and I discussed driving the following day to see Dara, as she lived on the water. Mary decided that the three and one half hour drive would be too tiring and she would rather just ride over to St. Augustine.

We awoke early the next morning and began making plans for the day. Suddenly, Mary announced that she thought she would like to go see Dara after all. Ft. Walton is not too far from Pensacola where my son, Barry and his wife, Melissa and their two girls, Sydney and Claire lived. I'm not sure how Barry found out we were coming, but he called to tell us that Melissa had a beach volleyball game in Navarre. Now, Navarre is about half way between Ft. Walton and Pensacola. Barry suggested that we come have dinner with them on the beach and watch Melissa play ball. We did. Mary (along with her son, Hayden and daughter, AJ), Dara, Dan (Dara's husband), and I joined Barry and his family.

Barry had dangerously high cholesterol levels. It concerned me at dinner when he asked, "Well, should I eat healthy, or should I order what I want?"

I wanted to tell him to eat healthy, but his sister and others at the table laughed and said, "Eat what you want and enjoy it!" He did. I don't recall what he ordered, but the meat was covered in melted cheese and, I believe, french fries to boot. It felt as though my heart just sank.

For most of their married life Melissa had been really good about cooking healthy meals. However, it seemed more and more that Barry got into cooking pork roasts, Boston Butts, and other fatty meats on the grill. Anytime I was passing through Pensacola on my way to Colorado, or was just out there and met him for lunch, he selected very high fat, delicious foods from the menu. So, you see, it wasn't just that meal that concerned me; I feared he was eating high cholesterol foods often. He worked all day at his office and, I feared, often grabbed lunch in town.

Soon after having eaten, Melissa and another woman with whom she was partnered, played the tournament as we all watched. Melissa played volleyball in high school and at Bradenton Junior college in Sarasota. She was quite good and took it very seriously.

When the tournament was over, Barry, Melissa, Mary and their girls played for a good while on the beach. Soon it became dark and the "party" had to end. We all said our good-byes, hugged and went our separate ways.

Mary, her children and I went back to Dara's to spend the night. The next morning was hectic as we wanted to get back to Live Oak as soon as possible. We got up, took our showers, cleaned up the guest house and began our journey back to Live Oak. Little did I know that the evening before would be the last time I would EVER hug my son.

4

THE DAY THAT CHANGED
OUR LIVES FOREVER

ON AUGUST 1, 2017 WE RETURNED HOME mid to late afternoon. Mary, her sisters and their husbands decided to go over to their Daddy's to visit him. I spent some time at home cleaning house, but had since sat down to watch T.V. for a little while. Sometime between 8:30 or 9:00, I guess, the girls drove up to the front of the house. As they came through the door, the look on their faces told me something was wrong. Melahn had the same look on her face, though more of a dazed look, that she had the evening she walked down the isle of Parkview Baptist Church in Lake City (where I had gone to services following a Christian Singles meeting I had attended), in short shorts and a casual shirt. The instant I happened to look back and see her I knew something was terribly wrong. I was terrified that something had happened to one of the children then. When we reached the church foyer, she told me Papa (my father) had been found dead sitting in his truck at the hospital. So, on this day, I knew the instant she came into the house this evening on August 1st, that something was dreadfully wrong. I had gotten up to greet the girls. They walked on in, all very somber. Melahn, my oldest, said, "Sit down, Mama. I have to tell you something. It's bad"

My heart was pounding by that time, like a drum. I anxiously asked, "What?" My first thought was that their daddy had died (he had a lot of heart related issues and heart surgery), or feared something had happened to one of the grandchildren. I guess what she had to say was, at the moment, the farthest thing from my mind. After all, Melissa had just texted all of us pictures of Barry playing volleyball.

Right then and there I heard the words I had so feared and yet thought God would never allow a situation for those words to be heard. Ever so quietly, Melahn's words were uttered, words that would crush everything in me, "Barry's gone."

I asked, "What do you mean he's gone?" When she repeated, the words…I knew.

My first reaction was, "NO!" I just kept repeating those words, no…no…no! The words became mingled with bitter sobs which turned into crys. When I finally got myself halfway together, I said, "I have to go…I have to go to Pensacola right now!"

Melahn, though I know her heart was breaking, remained relatively calm and told me we should all throw a suitcase together and get in the car. That we did. Our trip to West Florida began. I can only remember begging God all the way there…for at least 4 hours…to bring him back…to please bring him back…revive him…please revive him!

CHAPTER
5

UPON ARRIVAL

ALL OUR EMOTIONS WERE HIGH. OF COURSE, Melissa, his wife (now his widow) and the girls were still in shock. They were grieving, but holding up, so to speak. Melissa was being strong for the girls. All I could think about was getting to the funeral home. It was late, but I asked Melissa to call them to let them know we were coming and to ask one of them, any of them, to take me to the funeral home. I didn't want to tell Melissa or my daughters why. I felt desperate to put my hands on him and pray for him to be revived BEFORE he was embalmed! The funeral home denied me that right. Melissa said they did so, they told her, because (according to them) I would not want to see him as he was.

They refused me that desperate need. I wanted to go anyway and knock on the door. None of the family would take me up there. That broke my heart. They didn't understand. Jesus brought Lazarus back to life, he could bring Barry back. Jesus could restore oxygen to his brain…He had that power. I couldn't tell them my desperate hopes. Melissa was a nurse and I was sure she would tell me it was impossible at this point. I was sure my girls would support that. It still hurts that I wasn't even allowed to try. We sat and talked a lot that night.

I had given up the hope that I could pray over him. By this time, I just wanted to know what happened. It seems that they had played volleyball earlier and had returned home. Melissa had even texted me a picture of him playing. He appeared to have been playing quite vigorously.

The older daughter, Sydney, was attending Pensacola College and was not home at the time. The younger daughter was in high school and was getting ready to go out with friends. Melissa was cooking supper. While she was cooking, Barry, even though he had commented that he didn't feel good, decided to go out to the gym (set up in the garage area) and work out.

As the story was related to me, Claire came into the kitchen to grab a bite. She then told her mom she was leaving (for the plans she had to go to the movies). Her mom, thereupon, instructed Claire to go out to the gym and let her daddy know where she was going and with whom she was going. As she approached the gym, she saw her dad collapsed between two pieces of equipment.

Immediately, she ran to get her mom. Her mom yelled at her to call 911 while she, being a nurse, tried to resuscitate him. She was unable to, but kept trying (I understand) until the paramedics got there. They used their instruments and methods for resuscitating, including shock (I was told), but nothing worked. Melissa estimated that he might have been out there for about 20 minutes alone. It could have happened when he first went out, or later. We will never know. At first, the doctors said it was a massive heart attack. Later, a paramedic speculated that it could have been an embolism, as he turned blue so quickly.

At this point, we all had to accept that he was gone and wasn't coming back. So many questions rushed to my mind. Some of those questions, I kept to myself in an effort to nurse my own grief and not add to theirs. The odd thing is...and perhaps not so odd...we wished to see each other suffer as little as possible, we found ourselves saying the things that comfort each other rather that blurting out our pain and the hard questions. Someone said God had a reason and He just wanted Barry with Him. We talked about the part his high cholesterol and blood pressure might have played. We analyzed and analyzed.

Finally, I told Melissa that if I had not pushed him so hard to stop taking statins (he did once, briefly) and not to take them again, maybe he would be alive. She assured me that they had researched thoroughly and had discussed the side effects and weighed the research and it was his decision, and hers (one they made together) not to...even though, he had told the doctor to give him 3 months to get it down by himself and if he couldn't, he would take them. If I remember correctly, he had about a month to go. She very kindly insisted it was not my fault and reiterated that it was his time to go and God took him...for some reason we can't under-stand, God wanted him. Melissa and Barry shared a strong faith in God and in their Savior, Jesus Christ.

A million things pass through one's mind at a time like this. I recall that I mentioned to Melissa to make sure the girls never blamed God, or resented Him for taking their dad. I knew that the last thing Barry would have wanted was for Melissa or the girls (or any of his family) to be angry with God. She assured me that was important to her, too. I hoped and prayed that the girls would never blame their dad for leaving them. In my heart, I knew that God's decisions were perfect, even if we could not understand them. His wisdom far exceeds ours. He knows the future, we don't.

Within the first few hours, your mind feels like a spinning wheel. If only he had taken better care of himself. If only you had shared health information you had read, even though they didn't want to hear it. If only you had been there. You think of one "if only," after another. Finally, to your sorrow, you find that not one of them can bring him back.

One thing my girls, Melissa, Sydney and Claire all agree on was that we were so thankful God gave us all the indication anyone could ask for that Barry was saved and was right now, face to face with Jesus.

CHAPTER

6

THE FUNERAL: BORN FOR THIS PURPOSE

BORN FOR THIS PURPOSE...IT HAS TAKEN over two years to become reconciled to this reality. I've had mental battles with myself and sessions with the Lord over the age old questions a Christian has with the loss of any loved one, but especially when that one is taken from this earth at a young age, leaving behind a wife and teenage children. As I began thinking back over Barry's life, and I thought of all the times God intervened when death might have been staring Barry in the face, all the dangers he encountered (some not even related in this book) and the many times God spared him, those thoughts plagued me… the thought that he was born for this purpose. The account of his funeral service below and many others covered in the pages of this book, I believe will bear out my feelings.

The count, I heard, coming from those who were in attendance at the funeral (and should have had eyes closed and heads down, but peeked) was **at least** 10. That's the number of people who raised their hands that they accepted Christ that day…at the funeral!

You see, it wasn't an ordinary funeral. Knowing Barry's heart for, and deep commitment to soul-winning, Barry's wife, Melissa, asked the pastor, Dr. Ted Traylor to preach a soul-winning /salvation message. He went a step further. Near the end of the service, he actually invited any who felt led to do so, to say the sinner's prayer with him.

Time, then, was allowed for all who so desired, to say something about Barry. Perhaps they had funny stories to tell, or perhaps some personal experiences with him that enriched their lives. Others told of their admiration for him and of certain accomplishments they knew of. Dillon Harrell, Barry's nephew had some quite touching remarks. Barry's sister, Sherri, told several funny stories of childhood.

A highlight of this moment in time, was the reading of a letter, by his daughter, Sydney, which she had written for him. It was quite touching. In fact, some people requested a copy to use in teaching their children as well. In her reading, Sydney told how her dad would come up to their rooms at night and pray with them over their future husbands. (She didn't mention it in the letter, but Barry told me a few weeks before, that he was studying the book of Proverbs with the girls). Isn't it strange, I thought, how he had prepared them so well for a life without him, even though, as far as anyone knew, he had no idea the Lord was about to take him.

It was at this point that Brother Traylor offered (carefully and diplomatically), an opportunity... making clear that he would not embarrass anyone, and was not pressuring anyone...but, if anyone was willing, for those who said the sinner's prayer with him and truly accepted Christ as Savior...he would like to see a show of hands. As I said earlier, someone there reported at least 10 hands. There could have been others who did not wish to raise their hands. If God allowed Barry to look down at his services from Heaven, I know he felt great exhilaration at the souls coming to the Lord that day.

Souls that were on their way to hell, but because they came to services, because they wanted to show respect for Barry and his family, that eternal future trip was shifted from Hell to Heaven!

He was remembered well by friends and family. At the time, it seemed like more of a reunion than a funeral. It just did not seem real. Friends and family met at Barry's and Melissa's home prior to the funeral and following the funeral. To the amazement of our family, Olive Baptist of Pensacola, provided more food than one can imagine and for about a week. They kept bringing fresh food. Nothing seemed real, though. I couldn't eat for the first three days. I think I felt that if Barry couldn't, I wouldn't. Then, someone said to me, "Barry is up there enjoying a feast we can't even imagine. He would not want you down here depriving yourself for him." I went into the kitchen and fixed a plate.

CHAPTER

7

AFTER THE FUNERAL AND MELISSA'S WISDOM

LATER, AT MELISSA AND BARRY'S HOUSE... after the funeral service in Pensacola (interment was to be in Live Oak with a graveside service, there), I guess, as most grieving family members would do, we engaged, once again, in conversation as to why this might have happened. What went wrong? I mentioned to Melissa, in speaking of the matter, "Why did God allow our Barry to be taken, why didn't He intervene, as He had done so very many times before?"

Continuing with my questions and speculations, I asked Melissa if it could have been that, perhaps that God wanted some certain person, maybe a business associate, or someone else who would never have been in church, or perhaps never would have heard a salvation sermon, would never have come to Christ, had it not been for Barry's funeral, to be saved?

Then, in my confused, cluttered mind, my next thought was... and I shared with my daughter-in-law, the thought...if Barry had known, if God had spoken and said, "You can stay here, be at both daughter's graduations (one had graduated), one day walk them down the isle, see your grandchildren someday, OR, I can take you now and there will be souls saved and on their way to heaven (saved from an eternity in a burning hell). What is your decision? I asked her, "What do you think Barry would have said?"

I went on to say that I suspected Barry would have, with his heart breaking, told God to go ahead and take him. However, who could be sure of that. What a horrible decision that would have been! Melissa answered...very quietly and wisely..."That's why God doesn't ask us." What a very wise woman my son married. She was such a comfort during that time. Her answers were filled with a heaping serving of common sense.

Those first two or three days, especially during the funeral, with people gathering at the home, attending services, and with family and friends bringing food in...just the crowds that gather... none of it seemed quite real then, at that time, and is still to some extent, a blur.

At the time, I satisfied myself that the purpose for my son's death was for a greater purpose than I could understand. But, reminded myself that I must not be angry with God. I must not blame God. I could blame myself for reasons stated earlier...discouraging prescription medications, not, somehow convincing him to take natural nutrients that were touted to lower cholesterol and to take vitamins to build his health. I could blame Barry for not taking better care of himself. Or, I could accept that our days are numbered and it was his time to go. Each time I tried to accept the latter, I would be reminded of the scripture my mother always quoted to me that we could, "...lengthen or shorten our days. " I believe she deduced that from Proverbs, 3: 1-2, also Proverbs 9:11 and Proverbs 10:27. Without having ordered an autopsy, we will never know what caused Barry's death. I believe it is natural to speculate. It does not accomplish anything, but the emptiness and desperation one feels brings about the need to search for answers, asking questions which have no answers. In the earlier stages of grief one's mind tends to spin like a tornado with "if onlys" and "what ifs."

CHAPTER
8

BARRY'S GROWING UP YEARS

I HOPE A GRIEVING READER CAN SOMEHOW relate to what I have to share, here, about my son's life. Perhaps the reader can see God at work and more greatly understand their own situation and find peace and comfort. My hope is that someone bearing this burden of grief can look back upon their lost one's life and see where God was at work when you didn't realize a course was being charted.

To fully understand my thought processes, the conclusions I have drawn, my heartaches and my joys, you would need to know characteristics of the son I raised, at least to some extent, as I knew him. A reader would have to know at what point I can see, as I look back, God's many interventions, the influences I believe the Lord used to bring Barry to the point at which the Lord took him from this earth. For that reason, I am including information leading up to Barry's birth and high points of his life.

In retrospect, I believe that I was destined to rekindle an acquaintance (we "liked" each other in 5th grade) with Barry's father, which led to a romance and marriage. An onlooker might say that all the wrong reasons brought me back to Live Oak. My growing up dream in life and on into young adulthood, was to become a country singer. When I met my first love, I put my dreams on hold. My first love, after our break-up at North Florida Junior College a couple of years before, was seriously dating someone else in Live Oak (while I, now, was a student at Florida State about to graduate). Upon graduation, I felt an urgency to return to Live Oak. I thought my returning would interfere with any thoughts he might have had to marry her. He married her anyway! I now believe God arranged that. Only the combination of genes that God had planned could have produced Robert Barry Roberson.

Meanwhile, I had taken a job teaching in Live Oak. My ninth grade class was to present the Christmas program that December and rehearsal was underway at the old junior high auditorium (the only auditorium, and used by the high school also). Jimmy (Barry's father) came in with his brother and some friends and sat directly behind me. I knew he had married right out of high school, so when he asked for a date, I looked at him (likely a disdainful look). He leaned up and said, "You know I'm divorced, right?" I let him know that I had no idea. He persuaded me to ride around for a while after practice. His sad story of her leaving him for someone else and taking his two children really got to me. We continued dating for a couple of months, struck up a romance, then decided to get married. I think I had been hurt so previously and perhaps wanted to be in love again. Little did I know that the Lord wanted a little boy to be born who would have those particular genes (great athletic ability and strength) and experience the hurt and the joy at times, the disappointments, and the victories he would experience during his lifetime to mold him into the person he would become. It wasn't only Barry whom God arranged this union for, but my three girls, Melahn, Sherri, and Mary who are all unique each in her own way, and because of their same experiences, along with the genetic make-up that shaped who they would become, they have made contributions to God's work, also.

It is my belief that the Lord planned this course before the beginning of time. My son's time on this earth was part of a great plan God had for him.

9

INTRODUCING THE SHORT YEARS OF BARRY'S LIFE

WITH GREAT JOY ON THE EVENING OF JUNE 17, 1971, I heard the doctor announce, "It's a boy:" I had two girls already, precious and beautiful... now I had my boy! We named him Robert Barry Roberson after my father and Jimmy's grandfather.

As our third child, Barry grew to be a beautiful little blue eyed blond fellow. He was rather quiet and shy as a little guy. However he was not to be the last. A little over one and 1/2 years later, his third sister entered the world. Mary would prove to be a rather feisty little thing and somewhat of a challenge as a baby sister!

My children, later, suffered the heartbreak of a broken home, though not with the severity with which some children suffer…at least not in the early childhood stage. Their dad was rarely home except sometimes on Sunday afternoons (by his choice). The local Elk's Club and bars seemed to have had a magnetic effect on him. The children were used to spending most of their time with me.

Following the divorce, although I was teaching school, I often worked a second job to make ends meet. Naturally, that took some toll on the children. Many Saturdays were absorbed by my jobs. For several months, one school term, I worked after school on a homework hotline the school board established for children needing assistance with homework in the evenings. Sometimes, I maintained a summer job.

I raised my children alone, for the most part, though they had the love, devotion and good influence of my mama and daddy. My parents often kept them while I worked. They affectionately called them Granny Liz and Papa. The country singer, Randy Travis, captured the relationship between my daddy and my son in his song, "I Thought He Walked on Water," to the extent that it was almost a parallel. Daddy taught Barry to ride and rope and work cows. As head of the Sheriff's posse, Daddy would ride his horse in all the parades at the head of the horse lineup and carry the American flag. Daddy would saddle up the little white horse he let Barry claim, Tippy, and Barry would ride along beside him from about 4 years old until around 12 when sports took first place among his passions. I greatly credit my mama and daddy with building Christian character within all 4 of my children. I kept them in church and encouraged them to take part in youth activities. I played a lot of sermons in the car on tapes and CDs, but my mama drummed scriptures into them. At her funeral (after they were all grown and married) they gathered around the piano at Friendship Baptist Church and sang, "I Learned About Jesus in Grandma's Rocking Chair." They were joined by Mama's other two grandchildren, Shawn and Selena Roberts, children of my sister, the late Robbie Holmes Roberts and the late Julian Roberts.

Barry accepted the Lord at 9 years old and he never forgot that experience. Someone from our church went through the "Roman Road" with him and another youngster in Barry's bedroom one evening.

My son was always a loving child, but had a more serious tone than many boys his age. He was always a deep thinker. When he was having bad stomachaches once, and no medical reason could be found, I took him to a specialist. The specialist, almost in disbelief, told me that he had never had a teenager who was troubled by the issue Barry related to him. He said Barry was worried...very worried... about someone very close to him going to hell! The doctor was confused, but I completely understood. It was during his teenage years that one of his friend's mothers, a counselor at the high school, commented to me that her daughter recognized and talked about Barry's capacity for sensitivity toward their problems and concerns, not his own so much. I had known, in teaching, children characterized, by their parents, as sensitive and wanted me to treat them with "kid gloves" so to speak, but it was always because *their* feelings were easily hurt...not concern for other children! Of course, what that counselor shared just filled my heart with joy!

At home, Barry was called the "Golden Child" by his sisters. I waited on him, being the "man of the house" as my mother had waited on Daddy and as I had waited on their dad. It was just somehow ingrained in those of my generation, that the " men folks" were catered to. However, I always told him not to expect a wife to do for him as I did, especially if they both worked. Let me pause to say that the first time I saw him in his home after he married, I walked into the house and he was ironing his own pants! His sister, Sherri, likes to tell how, when she saw this upon a visit, she handed him her blouse and told him to do "this" too while he was at it. She said he politely handed it back with a chuckle and responded with, "You can iron your own things!" After that, I saw him iron his girl's clothes for church, as well as his own. He often grilled and helped with cooking.

As far as the childhood years, Barry (my third child) and his three sisters, Melahn (oldest), Sherri (second child), and Mary (the baby) would often fight, as children do. Of course, all the while creating memories they would grow to laugh about as adults .They were making memories that would become more dear than we could have imagined.

Let us fast forward to Barry's teenage years. In order for the reader to understand Barry's adulthood, the reader would need to have a glimpse of his teenage years. These were the years, in retrospect, that I see the many times God answered my prayers for intervention. Barry's dad worked hard on the farm all day, but as explained earlier, was seldom home...sufficient to say. Again, as I explained earlier, things escalated and the children's dad and I were divorced. Barry was four years old at the time. I tried not to speak ill of their dad to the children, as I felt they should respect both parents as much as possible. The years passed too quickly.

The summer preceding Barry's senior year of high school, in August, his grandfather died suddenly, with a stroke, or a heart attack. It was not established which. Talk about throwing someone for a loop! Barry was torn apart... devastated! His anger almost consumed him. Following the funeral, Barry got out of the car, went over to his Papa's truck, slammed his fist into it and screamed, "I want my Papa back!"

He had always fought a little and had experimented with alcohol in his junior year of high school, but both became more frequent. He became more aggressive on the football field. Upon striking out in baseball, he would slam his fist into the concrete wall (he was benched for this once). Needless to say, though the football coach seemed ok with increased aggressiveness; the baseball coach was often upset with him. The alcohol, also, became a great concern for his baseball coach. Still, Barry went to church and was able to maintain a good standing with teachers and friends. He graduated with honors. Though some of his friends worried about him, they all loved him through it all. He was well respected by most of his teachers and friends. They did not know what "drove" him, but I did.

Most of Barry's high school years he and the team were blessed with an exceptional football coach. He took this team to 2 consecutive State Championships. Those were glory days for the guys. Excitement was in the air and the whole town of Live Oak celebrated, heavily supported the team and many of the towns citizenry went to the State playoff games and the State championship game (though over 300 miles away, the bleachers were filled). Yes, our boy had some moments of great joy during those days. Just so the reader will know, the team after Barry and his buddies graduated, also won at State. Suuwannee High School, with coach Pittman, had 3 consecutive state championships!

The anger and inner rage, though at a lesser degree, continued beyond his senior year. Yet, as he progressed through his college days, it lessened more and more. He realized, as he related to me, that his drinking had caused a lot of his problems in high school and he, alone, caused the loss of his dreams. He had dreams of playing baseball at a major college. He was removed from the baseball team, just before the last two games, for drinking (not by the coach's choice, but by administration). He was blessed with the ability to see reality for what it was. His thinking matured more with each passing day. I used to pray that if my children were doing anything they shouldn't be doing, that God would let me know about it. My girls used to tell me that Barry wasn't doing anything the other guys were not doing, but he always got caught! I guess the Lord was answering my prayer, because his issues were ALWAYS called to my attention!

I will interject here that he had a high school sweetheart and the two of them seemed to be very much in love. Following high school, she would attend college many miles away, while he would stay near our hometown. Her folks had moved to South Florida during her senior year, though she remained with friends in Live Oak until graduation. Then she left to join them. She will be mentioned again about the end of his college days and as he sets out on life's journey as an adult.

All this was guiding him and forging his future to take him to the place where God wanted him, I now believe.

10

COLLEGE DAYS

THOUGH HE HAD SEVERAL CONTACTS FOR football scholarships, including Liberty University, Citadel, and Annapolis, he did not want to go terribly far off and did not want to go military. Then, I did not want him that far away, nor at the military academy. I would have loved him to have had the religious influence of Liberty, but, again, it was so far away. After all, he was my only boy and next to the baby! God was arranging my thinking and his, I fully believe.

A scholarship was granted to Barry by Valdosta State College (later to become Valdosta State University). He was granted a scholarship in Baseball and Football. His anger began to taper off, but still flared upon occasion. His broken heart followed over the loss of his Papa and the separation of him and his girl. Great adjustments were to be made. Because of the distance separating him and the girl, he did go out with other people and with his buddies. He sometimes got into fights on weekends in local clubs. He continued drinking. His dream was to play professional baseball, but he threw his arm out before one of the last games when scouts were to be there. In high school and college, it seems that the Lord blocked those dreams. He was awarded Most Valuable Player in baseball his Senior year at Valdosta State, so he had potential.

The following college story, I will tell only because it shows one more time when God intervened. The two sports kept him pretty busy. The anger seemed to subside more and more. He had lots of friends in high school and college with whom he laughed and had fun, but the alcohol had become a habit. He was in a club one night when a fight broke out. I will tell this story as it was told to me by his date and one of his closest friends. Barry and his friends were not involved in this particular fight. The police came, broke it up and left. Meanwhile, two undercover cops heard about it on their radios and decided to go check it out. It just happened that as one of the "fighters" was leaving, he decided to take a punch at Barry's friend who was standing at the bar minding his own business. Immediately, Barry took out after the boy. The boy ran out through the front door with Barry close behind. As Barry ran out, he ran into one of the plainclothed, undercover policemen. The fight had already been taken care of. The two came as "Johnny come latelies." They grabbed him and, not knowing who they were, he threw them off. They both jumped on him. They said they were taking him in. Whereupon he said, "You are not taking me anywhere until you tell me what I've done?" One put a 357 magnum up against his face, while the other handcuffed him. It was my understanding that neither of them identified themselves prior to this action. That upset me more than one can imagine, upon hearing the story. What if another person had run by and hit the policeman's arm? The gun could have gone off and killed Barry. This was more confirmation for me, as I look back, that GOD HAD A PLAN for Barry and nothing could have killed him at that time. However, these were heavy expenses incurred for a single mom, as it took a lawyer to get him freed. He never went to court. Also, a DUI during the college days increased the financial load. He was cleared, but at a price, with a lawyer involved. I knew of no more fights after that. I repeated the former comment to his oldest sister after that incident, "You remember I told you I have always prayed that if one of my children was doing something they shouldn't do, God would let me find out...well, with your brother that's becoming an expensive prayer!"

I recall his sister, Melahn, once again, reminded me of the comment she had made when he was in high school. She said, "I told you before, Mama, Barry isn't doing anything that most of his friends aren't doing, but he is the only one that always gets caught." Again, now I know that God was still working in his life, even then. God was continuing to answer my prayers!

Yes, even those days were used to serve a purpose. In years to come, conversations about those days brought my son and me closer. He told me, after those college days, how sorry he was for the grief, not to mention the money he cost me. In fact, in years to come, he repaid all of the lawyer expenses, but what meant the most was the appreciation he expressed concerning the fact that no matter how meager my finances, I always found a way to go to almost all of his baseball and football games, whether in or out-of-state. What he didn't know was, at that time, one of the greatest joys of my life was watching him play ball. That was not to minimize the great joy my girls have brought me over the years. Yes, those expenses always tormented Barry and, as I mentioned above, in years to come, he insisted on paying me back. He was a good son.

I will share one comical experience during baseball season. I got a call from Coach Thomas. He asked if Barry walked in his sleep. Caught off guard, and not thinking, I said no, I didn't think so. I learned he had found Barry asleep in the hallway on a trip out-of-town, and just assumed he had sneaked out, gotten drunk (which that surprised me, as he was usually responsible when the team was depending on him) and had fallen asleep in the hallway. He was suspended from one game. As I was telling one of his sisters, she said, "Mama! Don't you remember how we couldn't even open our bedroom door some mornings because Barry was asleep in the hallway against our door?! Yes, I did remember then. It happened several times. I never got back with coach on that one, but I knew deep inside that was what had happened. I was pretty sure my son would not sneak out on a road trip. And, as I said, Coach Thomas did award Barry a trophy his senior year as MOST VALUABLE PLAYER!

Finally, the college days came and went. His high school sweetheart met someone else, married her new love and broke Barry's heart. However, soon the Lord would open new doors that would make all the hurt seem a blur of the past.

11

A NEW LIFE BEGINS

FINALLY, THOSE COLLEGE DAYS WERE OVER, as were his glory days of football and baseball. Graduation day... and Barry began his REAL life. He became affiliated with the Frier Corporation in mobile home sales. Just prior to moving up in the company, he met what was to become his true and lasting love and later his beloved wife, Melissa Rewis.

All those former heartaches from high school and college slipped into oblivion when he saw Melissa walk onto the mobile home lot where he had begun to work the summer after graduation. He related to me and anyone else who would listen, how he said to the guys upon seeing her, "That's the girl I'm going to marry!" AND, he did. I had never seen him as happy since his high school football team won their first State Championship game! Seriously, she was the answer to prayer. Whatever hurt and anger was once harbored in his heart, seemed to fade away.

Barry and Melissa dated for a couple of years. During that time, one of his best friends from childhood, Matt, became CEO, in effect, of his dad's large mobile home dealership chain and Barry was granted a partnership on the Pensacola lot and a management position over several other lots in Florida and Alabama. He was on his feet and doing well.

Next came the big decision to marry. The two had a beautiful wedding at Olive Baptist Church in Pensacola, which they had been attending for most of the two years. If memory serves, they had joined this church at some point during the two years. The business was blessed and success ensued, which was a good thing, because a little less than a year later their first child, a daughter, Sydney Nichole Roberson was born.

That first child had medical complications at birth. I watched my son sit at that hospital and hold her every minute he was allowed. If she was hooked up to a machine, he kept his hand on her hour after hour. Melissa, too, as soon as she was able was right beside her daughter and her husband. God answered prayer and the defect healed itself through the hand of God.

About three years later, their second daughter was born to these brave and proven faithful parents. God blessed them with a healthy baby girl. They named her SarahLynn Claire Roberson.

The ensuing years were good years for Barry and Melissa, and their two girls. The girls began early in athletic endeavors. Both Sydney and Claire settled into volleyball and both became exceptional in their chosen sport. Those were wonderful years and Mom and Dad were faithful to "be there" for their daughters. They had many proud moments watching their girls grow and watching their successes both academically and in sports. Their mother was an avid volleyball player in school, and college. Both girls were to later attend college on volleyball scholarships. You know their dad's sports history, so it is no surprise that the girls are fine athletes.

Their lives were exceptionally blessed. Then for reasons we can't know on this earth, God intervened. He took our Barry from his loving family, leaving one daughter during her first year in college and one, I believe, about to begin her junior year in high school. Both continued, for a time, with the volleyball. Claire struggled her last 2 years of high school knowing that her dad would no longer be among the spectators. Sydney, likewise, missed her dad as she went on to continue playing college ball. He was there for her first season, only.

I began this chapter with the title, "A New Life Begins." The rest of this chapter will revert back to the big change in Barry's life which brought him to an unusually close relationship with Christ. This might be a bit of backtracking, but it will explain the impact he came to have on others in his life.

Barry and Melissa placed a strong emphasis on having their girls and themselves in Sunday school and church. A few years into their lives together, they both became Sunday school teachers. I'm not saying they had a fairy-tale marriage (though in many ways, they did). They had disagreements and both spent moments pouting. Yet, by-and-large, it was an exemplary marriage.

Only one cloud was hanging. This was a carryover from their college days and early adulthood. They were not heavy drinkers, but when sports connected friends came over, they would participate in the beer drinking thing. At times, Barry would have a couple of beers at night before retiring for the night. He always said he could take it or leave it and that it was not a problem. Then he called me one night about four or five years before we lost him on earth, to tell me of an experience he had. He said he was talking to his oldest daughter now in high school. He was telling her he hoped she would not drink with friends, and not ride with friends drinking. He explained how it lowered inhibitions and impaired judgement. Her response was, "Oh Daddy, I'm gonna drink when I get older. I see how much fun you and Mamma have with your friends!"

That response hit him hard. He related how he had gone to his office early the next morning ahead of everyone else. He said he fell on his knees by the wall and cried out to the Lord. Barry told God that he could not quit drinking on his own. He told the Lord that when the time was right, He (GOD) would have to take it away. At this point, Barry said, "Mama, I know we're Baptist and we don't believe that God speaks to you audibly, but I heard a voice say, 'The time is right now!' " Barry went on to explain that he didn't know if his mind was hearing it so strongly that he felt he heard it, but he heard it. " He went on to say that it felt like something pulled out of his back. The funny thing is, my daughter's father-in-law, when God cured him of leukemia, said he felt that pulling from his back, also. He was Baptist, too!

From that day until the day he left this earth, Barry never wanted another drink and was not tempted in the presence of others participating. Barry had always loved the Lord. He loved reading the scriptures. He was devoted to teaching the salvation plan to the middle schoolers at church. With this new victory, he became even more devoted to these things, but also became interested in mission work.

The opportunity soon presented itself for Barry and Melissa to go on a two week mission trip to Africa. The dream became a passion. There was one problem. The trip to Africa was very expensive and finances were an issue. It was the point in time when real estate sales were dropping and so were mobile home sales. Barry was now a partner on the Pensacola lot, but had given up trying to manage several other lots. That position kept him on the road early on in the marriage and Melissa was not happy with that. He put his family and their need for him above the larger income.

Again, the Lord came to the rescue. They had owned a little rental on Navy Point when the BP oil spill took place. Many homes near the water were compensated. BP had sent a check a year or so before and they thought that was all and thought no more about it. Suddenly, they got, in the mail, a significant check for further compensation. About the same time, they were having problems with their older SUV which would be rather expensive to fix. The car was parked in the drive beside a big tree when lightning struck and knocked out (I believe) the electrical system and perhaps other damage. The car was declared totaled and the insurance they received was more than an offer, previously given, for a trade-in!

The road was paved for the African mission trip. Barry and Melissa went on that trip and I babysat the girls. They were not sure of safety issues and chose not to take the girls on this trip. The two of them loved the experience and had hoped to go back there someday. That was not to happen for Barry. He left a legacy at that mission, though. Apparently influenced by missionaries of other religions, the leader of the group of churches with which Barry and Melissa were working, talked to Barry about one of his pastors telling his congregation that they had to pay into the church to be saved (this is my understanding of the situation as Barry explained it to me). He asked Barry his opinion. Barry explained to the leader that salvation is free and shared related scriptures (concerning grace). "Yes, Christians should support the church with tithes and offerings," Barry told him, but explained that salvation does not depend on that. If I understood my son correctly, this church leader stayed in contact for a long time leaning on Barry for advice and guidance. Since my son is no longer with us, here, I can only rely on memory of conversations with him. I just know that after our conversations, I felt so proud of him for his love for the church and the truth of the scriptures.

A second mission trip opportunity soon presented itself. About a year later, the couple decided to volunteer to go to an orphanage in Mexico. Though it was located in a very dangerous area, a bus with security took them to the location and provided safe entrance. They were told they must stay inside the compound, that it was not safe outside.

They did take the girls on this trip and the girls were also allowed to work with smaller children. They were teenagers by this time. As the Lord worked in all their hearts, the girls also became hooked on missions. Prior to the trip, Barry even attended a training camp with Claire. They had to live without modern conveniences and limited supplies. This was to prepare the youth for situations they might encounter in missions. Claire said it was tough, but they made it through.

The church was not the only place where Barry's influence became apparent. Yes, he engaged in witnessing to several friends and acquaintances, but he had begun a Bible study once a week at the mobile home lot with the employees and took that quite seriously.

Little did Barry, or any of us know his time was running out. We knew he had high cholesterol. He had been to his doctor with heart issues, but it was never recommended that he go through extensive testing, to my knowledge. Barry and Melissa often played on beach volleyball teams in the summer. Periodically, Barry would take advantage of the gym they had set up in one of the garages. Basically, his friends and family thought him to be generally healthy.

Early in this account of Barry's life, I spoke of the unusual circumstances that brought his baby sister, Mary (from Colorado) and me, along with Dara (his niece) and her husband, Dan, to Navarre (near Pensacola) for dinner with Barry and Melissa that evening before the Lord took him. I believe with all my heart, that was arranged by our loving God, our Lord and Savior, Jesus Christ. He arranged for the sister Barry seldom saw…had not seen in a year or two… and me to see and hug my son, her brother, one last time.

Life and the events of life often take us by surprise, but you do find one day that you are gradually becoming preoccupied with other things in life once more. I well remember that, in the beginning, I thought I never would. Feelings, with which, I am sure, you, the reader, can identify. It took about two years for me to realize that feeling guilty and like I was betraying my son if I had him off my mind for even a few minutes was keeping me "bound" and "unproductive" for the most part. There is no denying that those feelings never totally go away, but they do become less consuming.

CHAPTER

12

TRAIL OF GRIEF, HEARTACHES AND VICTORIES

THIS FINAL CHAPTER DETAILS MY JOURNEY through the effects of the loss of my son. It is designed to bring hope and blessings to others who are on that same journey. Above all, it is designed to bring honor and glory to the Savior, Jesus Christ, who held me close through it all, and is still holding me close.

In an earlier chapter, the reader was taken through the horror and immediate shock and ensuing grief at the news that Barry was gone. That chapter told of the times God spared him as a young man. This last chapter will deal with my memories of how God worked in my son's life, as they are revealed to me little by little and the thought processes as they entered my mind.

As the weeks passed, I was still trying to make sense of it all. Once when I was feeling unloved by God, I heard my heart cry out, "If you loved me how could you put me through this pain!?" It was almost as though the Lord was answering me in a conversation, because almost immediately the thought struck me that, yes, He loved me...but... those people who were saved at Barry's funeral...He loved them, too! Barry's salvation was secured, but only because of his funeral, perhaps, would those people have had their salvation secured! As stated previously, It was very likely that some of those people were there as business associates, various acquaintances, old friends, many not spiritual and might never have been exposed to God's Salvation Plan, had they not gone to show respect for Barry and his family. For a moment, I felt a twinge of bitterness, but then God reminded me of Barry's deep concern and his heart for the lost. The Lord did not stop at that. He reminded me that Mary once stood before an old rugged cross and looked upon her son, torn to shreds and aching beyond anything we could imagine. The Lord was merciful in taking Barry suddenly and without warning.

There was no telegram from an agent of the U.S. Government telling me my son was killed in action. God spared me the mental images of him lying there wounded, knowing he was dying without family, or friends, or any loved ones. What endless pain that must be for parents of sons and daughters who have fallen in battle! My son was surrounded by love until God had his angels transport him to the gates of heaven where he heard the Father say, "Well done my good and faithful servant. Enter into thy rest." I began to count my blessings.

Realizing all the thoughts, dwelling on all the unanswered questions cannot bring your child (or any loved one) back, that it can't eliminate the pain, you do come to realize. But, that strangely enough, it does bring an unusual kind of peace...the peace that surpasses all understanding.

There is comfort for Christian parents. As I explained to one of my granddaughters (for all saved people) the mind, soul, spirit...all that is the real us...all but the body which simply houses the person we are...our mind, soul, and spirit is transported, at the moment of death to the presence of our God and our Savior, to Heaven. Paul said to be absent from the body is to be present with the Lord.

We will always miss our loved one. Sometimes, there will be tears, sometimes we will remember something funny they did and find ourselves chuckling. You will, very likely, as I did, think at first it can never get better, you'll never stop crying. I can't promise it will get "better," but you will begin to adjust. You will begin to become absorbed in other things, in other children, in grandchildren and the grief will be less intense.

Above all, remember to thank God that He let you have this person in your life...if only for a little while. As I said earlier, my son was 46 years old on June 17th, just before the Lord took him on August 1st of 2017. Almost daily, I am so thankful for those 46 years. I praise God and Christ my Savior that my son, Barry Roberson, was in my life, that I have wonderful memories of him and his sisters fighting as they grew up (but loving each other dearly), all the ballgames from little league baseball and independent football to middle school baseball and football, to high school baseball and football, to College baseball and football and all the excitement of watching him play. I'm thankful for memories of his friends coming over and watching them play and tease each other. I'm thankful for memories of his junior and senior proms. God brought him through many ups and downs, but I am thankful for each of those life's experiences which molded and shaped him into the amazing son he became and the servant for Christ our Lord that he became.

PICTURES AND
OTHER ADDITIONS

Having a Big Time

Took him over to see my folks,
Daddy saddled up old Smokey
Joe... He came running in and said,
"Mama, I'm having a big time!"

To Disney World or a picture show,
And, his big smile would just thrill
me so, as he looked up and said,
"Mama, I'm having a big time!"

Big times come and big times go,
That's one thing we all know. From a
baby boy, I watched him grow... And,
time marches on that we can't slow.

From baseball hero to football champ, Life moves on and leaves its stamp... But, I knew he was having a big time!

Soon he met his own true love, God blessed him with from up above. Two little girls brought him such joy... Life was good for my little boy. And....I knew he was having such a big time!

His family grew and they loved the Lord. Their mission trips were their delight, to spread the gospel and shed its light. They made as many trips as they could afford... But now it seems when it rained, it poured!

At 46, God called him home. I heard his sister tell me, "Mama, he's gone." So sudden, and the grief is still so hard to bear. Yet, now when I look up into the great "SOMEWHERE"...Well... Good

**times come and good times go, and
there are some things that we can't
know... But I know he's with Jesus
and I can almost hear him say,**

**"Mama, I'm REALLY having a
big time!"**

This was written as a speech by my grand-daughter, Sydney Roberson, to give at her dad's funeral. She asked me to edit it, whereupon, I told her he would want her to say it just as she was speaking to a friend. I suggested that she should give it in her own vernacular, her Southern manner of speaking:

**Given by Sydney Roberson at her
father's funeral**

**In words written in red, in my dad-
dy's Bible, it says in the book of John,
Chapter 16, verse 33, "These things
I have spoken to you, that in Me
you may have peace. In the world
you have tribulation, but take heart**

for I have overcome the world." My dad came up to my room one night before I graduated high school and shared this verse with me. It has stuck ever since. My father was my rock and also my family's. He is the Godliest man I've ever seen in my entire life. I'm sure most of us can agree to that. He was the perfect example of how a husband and father should act. He would pray with me and my sister for our perfect husband that God had picked out for us. He would pray for our family and friends everyday.

In the mornings, when we all would get ready to go to school or work, me and Claire would accidently walk in on him kneeling beside his bed, praying before his day started. Me and Claire would look at each other and just say, "Oops," and speed walk out. The Holy Spirit constantly ran through my dad.

Everyone always called my daddy a legend when we would go home to Live Oak, which was my dad's home town. Apparently, while my parents were dating he even managed to get asked for his autograph! My sister and I gave him a hard time when we would hear that story, because how could our goofy dad be so cool? It was so weird when we would talk to kids or even adults in his home town and they'd say, "Barry Roberson is your dad?" and we would just respond with a drawn out "yeahhh??" because we didn't know if that was a good question or a bad one because in a small town like that everyone knew what you did whether you liked it or not. But, it was mostly good things.

My daddy was my hero. He said he never deserved what God gave him (and we don't), but my dad promised himself that he'd never take anything for granted again. The amount of love he had for my family was unconditional. To think that he loved our God more than he loved us, just blows my mind. There is nothing more I can say to define him. A God fearing man sums it up.

I love you, dad.

PHOTOS

Family time with their dad. Left to right (top) Sherri,
Jimmy, Mary, Melahn. (bottom) Barry

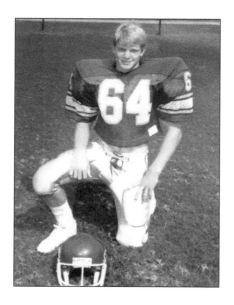

Barry played on Suwannee High School
Bulldog team. Won championship games
twice during his days there.

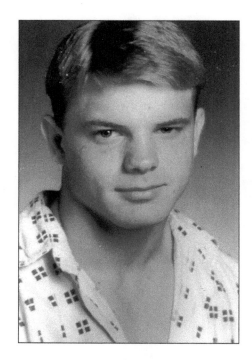

Barry as a student at
Suwannee High School

Playing for Valdosta State
College Baseball team.
Won trophy as Most
Valuable Player his senior
year. Now VSU.

Barry and Melissa
becoming one, joined in
holy matrimony

Mother and son
dance at Barry and
Melissa's wedding

Willing participants, all three sisters love Melissa

Busy or not, he always took time for his
beloved Granny Liz.

Barry and Melissa enjoy a visit from Keith and Sherri.
L to R: Keith, Sherri, Barry and Melissa.

The family is simply enjoying an outing

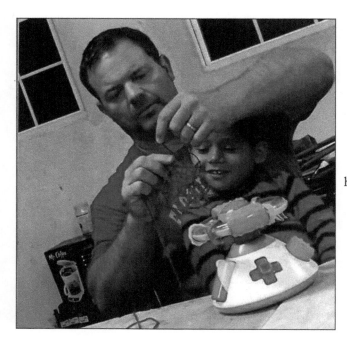

An incid
happened c
great bon
in these
Mission
to Mexi

A visit with their dad.
Pictured L to R: Melann,
Sherri, Jimmy (their
dad), and Barry

After dinner with Live Oak family at
the Brown Lantern. 2 months before the
Lord took him.

L to R, Sherri, Melahn and Barry not
long before he was gone

The two very m
in love. Few mo
before we lost

At sister, Melahn's house
in Live Oak. Family
gathering.

Beach volleyball tournament in Navarre. His last full day on earth. Sister, Mary and 2 of her children from Colorado. Dinner together for the last time.

Life must go on. This was taken approximately 2 years after their dad left us. Both are in college. Know he would want them

CPSIA information can be obtained
at www.ICGtesting.com
Printed in the USA
LVHW051558050121
675506LV00017B/932

9 781662 800528